Why

Not Sell?
20 Simple Fixes

Rayne Hall

CONTENTS

INTRODUCTION

Does your book sell as well as it deserves?

If it doesn't, one of twenty blocks may hinder its sales—blocks which can be easily removed once you're aware of them.

Each chapter reveals one area where indie authors are sabotaging their books' success, and shows how you can free yourself from that trap. The focus is on simple fixes, and actions you can take immediately, although sometimes I point out long-term strategies.

Whether you want to sell 100,000 copies or would be happy with just 100, this guide helps you raise your book above the hundreds of thousands of titles competing for attention.

Sometimes you'll experience a joyful 'aha' moment as you discover a new approach. At other times, you may cringe when you realise how your hard promotion work has been driving readers away. Be prepared for tough insights.

This book provokes. It turns advice you've read elsewhere upside down, and challenges what you think you know. You may not like it.

If a suggestion displeases you, feel free to skip it. I'm merely the consultant, you're the CEO. I advise, you decide.

This is not a 'Book Publishing 101' manual. It is a guide for authors who have indie-published (self-published) at least one book, and have already tried different marketing strategies, but not yet achieved success. If you've chosen the traditional publishing path or if you're still at the planning stage, it will be of limited use, although you may pick up pointers.

It also assumes you have written a great book. Your book need not please everybody—no book ever does—but unless it pleases the kind of people for whom you've written it, no marketing strategy can conjure up success.

I've made many mistakes, have learnt from them, and reveal them in this book. You don't need to make those mistakes if you learn from mine.

While I have sold a lot more books than most indie authors, bear in mind that I'm not one of the million-copy sellers. I can show you how to boost your sales from meagre to substantial, but I don't have a magic wand.

To avoid clunky phrases like 'he or she does this with him or her' I'm using female pronouns in some sections, male in others. The words, grammar and spelling are British English.

Now let's look at ways to propel your book to success.

Rayne Hall

CHAPTER 1: THE BOOK COVER

Your book cover is pretty, aesthetic, stunning—but it doesn't do its job.

Most book purchases—ebooks or print—happen online. The reader browsing sites sees a dozen or more books displayed on the page. Her eye scans over them, and unless one catches her attention, she clicks 'next', sees another page of covers, 'next' again, 'next', 'next', 'next'.

Your book cover has a fraction of a second to arrest the eye. Catching the casual browser's attention is the book cover's main function. Everything else counts for nothing if it fails at this stage.

Let's see if your cover lets you down, and if we can fix it.

IS THE DESIGN SYMMETRICAL?

Symmetrical designs—where the shapes on the right side reflect those on the left like a mirror— look beautiful and harmonious. But they don't attract attention. When several images are displayed on one page, the eye skips the symmetrical ones and lingers over the asymmetrical ones. Those hint at tension, excitement, a suspenseful read.

Here's an example I created. First, the nice but unexciting symmetrical version, then three quick asymmetrical variations, each of them more likely to catch the eye.

My friend, German comedy thriller author Chris van Harb, has given permission to include a 'before and after' of one of her real covers. On the left, you see the symmetrical (boring) version. I used the same stock photo to create an asymmetrical design, and tweaked several other details (text colour, fonts) at the same time.

The new cover coincided with a general dip in Amazon.de sales, so unfortunately Chris couldn't measure the effects. I would have loved to tell you what the actual boost in sales was.

Suggested Actions:

Crop the picture differently, so the main graphic element is off-centre.

Instead of centering title and author name, align one of them left, the other right.

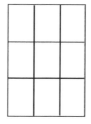

Use the 'Rule of Thirds' for the design. Image lines dividing your book into thirds horizontally and vertically, as shown above.

If possible, arrange the title on one of the two horizontal lines, and an arresting part of the picture where two lines cross. If the cover image is a close-up of a face, try to place the pupil of one eye on such a cross. This needs a bit of jiggling, but the effects are startling.

IS THE PICTURE TOO COMPLEX?

You may want the picture to reflect the complexity of the cover, showing several interesting characters in a detailed landscape. Perhaps you've paid an artist to paint everything just so, and are thrilled with the results.

However, there's simply too much for the eye to take in. The casual viewer's glance is arrested by simple images and passes over the complex ones. Remember, most books are sold online, and the covers are first seen in thumbnail size. With minute displays, the detail gets lost.

A character attracts the eye more than a landscape or an object. A portrait or half-body character (from the waist up) typically gets more attention than a full-body figure. At thumbnail size, a single character works better than a group, and a simple background better than a complex one.

Unless your book's genre requires several characters (for example, two men on the cover for gay romance), use just one. This is probably the main character, or the main character's love interest. With straight romance, a handsome hero on the cover helps sell the book.

In some genres, a simple object can work instead of a character if the design is right—for example, a pair of fashion shoes for a Chicklit novel about a shoe-loving fashionista.

Suggested Action:

Crop the picture, using just a part of it, to show a single character. You can use the other parts of the picture in your publicity materials, for guest posts and on your website.

Here's an example of a cover with too many characters, and a quick cropped version which is stronger:

DOES THE COVER HAVE TOO MUCH TEXT?

On paperbacks, several text elements (title, subtitle, series name, author name, contributors list, genre, tagline, endorsement) look great—but only when viewed at full size.

Nowadays, potential readers find their next book online. Whether it's an ebook or a paperback, they first see it at thumbnail size. The bits of text are so small, they're illegible. Instead of enhancing the cover, they make it look cluttered. The rapidly scanning viewer's eye passes over them.

Here's an example of a text-cluttered cover:

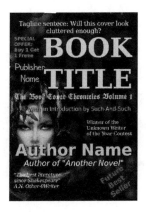

Two text elements (title and author name) are enough. Three often looks great, and this is a good solution if your book is also sold in bookshops. The third element may be a subtitle, the series title, the genre or a very short tagline. Four text elements can still work, but more than that, and the cover will probably fail.

Suggested Actions:

Remove superfluous text from the cover. If you (or your designer) have used Photoshop or GIMP, it's a simple matter of deleting some layers. Increase the size of the text elements you're going to keep.

IS THE AUTHOR NAME THE WRONG SIZE?

If you've bought your cover from an aspiring artist or newbie designer, the title and author name may be small, like captions for the picture. This makes them look timid, and timidity doesn't get attention.

Conversely, you may have blown your own name up to dominate the cover, in hopes of fooling readers that you're famous. An unknown name doesn't arrest the eye, and hides the elements that would.

Here the author's name is far too big and far too small:

Suggested Action:

Choose a font size that's smaller than the title, but big enough to read at thumbnail size.

DOES THE COVER SIGNAL THE WRONG GENRE?

Readers in search of a book typically look for their favourite genres, such as Paranormal Romance, Urban Fantasy or Chicklit. They have already read many books in this genre, and are conditioned to associate certain cover styles with it.

A cover which signals the genre whets their appetite, especially if the design reminds them of their recent favourite reads.

If your cover's picture and design don't signal the genre, eager book buyers will click on another cover that does.

Suggested Action:

Study book covers in your genre, especially the bestsellers of the past ten years. These are embedded in your potential reader's memory as great reads. Model your own cover on them to give your reader the visual cue that your book will offer similar pleasure. But don't copy the designs to the extent that the reader thinks she's already read this book.

IS THE PHOTO A DUPLICATE?

If you've used a stock photograph (licensed from an agency) or bought a ready-made cover (which utilises a stock photo), chances are, the same picture is already on someone else's cover. If potential readers see several books with the same picture in a list of suggestions, they'll assume—consciously or subconsciously—that the books are all the same.

Here's an example of what happens when several publishers use the same stock photo for the same kind of book:

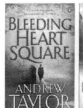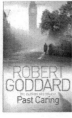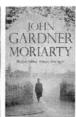

These books were published by some of the world's biggest publishers who had the resources to tinker with the background and change colours—but it's still blatantly the same photo.

Readers browsing online for a thriller would see these covers displayed side by side.

Some of these authors are famous with loyal fans who buy their latest book regardless of the cover. But other books with the same cover photo (published by small presses and indie authors) were doomed.

Suggested Actions:

Take your own photo, or hire a photographer if you can afford the fee.

Hire an artist to paint an original cover picture. This may be less expensive than you think, but it will take time.

Use the picture you have, but change it: flip it left to right, crop part of it, change the colouring, or merge it with another picture.

ARE THERE TOO MANY COLOURS?

Although people's colour perceptions vary, pictures with a narrow colour palette tend to draw the eye more powerfully. If your cover has a mix of red, white, black, blue, green, yellow, pink, orange and purple, the result may be cheerful and pleasing in close-up, but on a page of thumbnails, it will get overlooked.

A cover design in different shades of just one, two or three colours is a powerful magnet. For example, try shades of red and black, or blue and purple.

Suggested Actions:

Use your existing cover and manipulate the colours (or ask a Photoshop- or GIMP-savvy friend to do this for you).

Choose a colour scheme that suits the book's genre and mood.

DOES IT LACK CONTRAST?

Strong contrasts draw the eye. If your cover's text blends gently into the soft-hued picture, this can be a pleasure to see at full size. But it doesn't work for thumbnails competing on a page with others.

Effective contrasts are between light and dark, and between different colours.

Suggested Action:

Increase the contrast of your cover. Make some of the dark parts darker, some of the light parts lighter.

Choose a colour scheme with an intense contrast, for example, green-yellow-black or red-white.

CHAPTER 2: THE BLURB

The blurb (book description) on the book's back cover and online product page is the most important part of the book. Almost everyone reads or at least skims it before deciding whether or not to buy. It probably plays a bigger role in your sales than any other factor.

IS THE BLURB TOO LONG?

If the book description goes on and on, the reader gets bored—and looks at the next book in the catalogue instead.

Many authors load their book description page with a lengthy synopsis, subplots, commentary, author bio, purchased reviews and other material, in the hope that this will persuade the reader to become interested in the book. But the reader who visits your product page is already interested. Don't bore her away!

The description needs to stir the interest into an urgent desire to read the book, so the reader either clicks to get the free sample or to buy the book at once.

Suggested Action:

Shorten your blurb. Cut all superfluous material—you may be able to use it elsewhere in your promotions. Model your blurb's length on that of the bestsellers of your genre. 200-800 words is usually enough.

IS IT TOO COMPLEX?

In an attempt to do the book justice and reflect every nuance of content, writers often cram too much into the blurb. This leaves the reader confused.

Better to focus on one aspect of the book, and present that well. Keep it simple.

Unlike a synopsis, the blurb should not reveal the plot. Otherwise, the reader doesn't need to read the book to find out what happens.

A good blurb is a teaser. It presents an exciting situation that the reader can't resist.

Suggested Actions:

Keep it simple and get straight to the point.

For non-fiction, show what benefits the reader will get. (Example: *Writing Fight Scenes:* "Learn step-by-step how to create fictional fights which leave the reader breathless with excitement.") Add some key features of the content.

For a novel, focus on the main character's major goal and conflict. Leave out subplots, minor characters and all the enchanting details. Focus on the first couple of chapters of your book. Leave out anything that comes later.

Do you have a tagline, logline, elevator pitch or similar short teaser for the book? Flesh it out with a couple more sentences, and you'll have an irresistible blurb.

DOES IT FAIL TO GRAB?

Many blurbs leave the reader unmoved. Without emotional involvement, the reader doesn't feel compelled to read the story.

Suggested Actions:

Here's a powerful method to make the reader care. Start the blurb with the character's goal. Whatever the character wants or needs that sets the events in motion, state it. Example: "Debutante Arabella needs a husband."

Add the reason why, but without explanations. Simply reveal what's at stake or what the dire consequences of failure would be: "Debutante Arabella needs a husband, or her brother goes to prison."

If you can create a sense of urgency by mentioning a deadline, even better: "Debutante Arabella needs a husband, and she needs him by Christmas, or her brother goes to prison."

The sentence "[Character] needs [goal] before [deadline], otherwise [drastic consequences]" is an irresistible hook for any reader who enjoys the kind of story you've written.

Add another sentence creating an emotional dilemma: "But the only man she loves is betrothed to her best friend." Finish with a question. "How can she protect her brother without betraying her friend or her own heart?"

This gets the reader's imagination going, and she'll want to read the story.

IS IT WORDY AND WAFFLING?

Your writing style for the blurb needs to be exciting and punchy. Many blurbs are vague, clumsy, or cluttered with phrases that add no content.

Suggested Actions:

Give every sentence at least one vivid verb and specific noun, and scrap most adjectives and adverbs.

Avoid Passive Voice sentence structure ("When her son is killed by native warriors...") and use Active Voice where possible ("When native warriors kill her son...").

Delete phrases that carry no content ("This book is about..." "This story tells how..." "What happens next...")

Delete sentences in which the character thinks, considers, understands and realises things. Focus on the action.

Tighten the phrasing. Avoid "he starts/begins to" and "she finds herself". Instead of "He starts to plot revenge" write "He plots revenge." Instead of "She finds herself journeying into the jungle" write "She journeys into the jungle."

DOES IT LACK THRILL WORDS?

Every genre has certain words which send delicious thrills down the reader's spine and get her imagination going. They signal that this book contains the kind of story she loves.

In Regency Romance, words like 'ball, governess, rake, rogue, elopement, scandal' capture the reader's imagination, while for Westerns it may be 'stagecoach, sheriff, outlaw, hanging, posse, saloon' and for High Fantasy 'sword, wizard, enchanted, magic, prophecy, quest'. They act as an open-sesame.

If your blurb lacks the magic words, the reader will move on to look at another book.

Suggested Action:

Make a list of the thrill words of your genre (or genres, if your book straddles several). Choose the ones which fit your story and insert two or more into your blurb.

MISTAKES I MADE AND LEARNT FROM

For a short while, I believed the 'gurus' who urged authors to make blurbs as long as possible. I wrote 2000-

word blurbs and stuffed them with keywords. When book sales dropped instead of rising, I realised that readers don't want to read long blurbs. They want to read books.

CHAPTER 3: SAMPLE PAGES

Before buying, readers can click 'view inside' or 'download sample' to see if they like the book. Many download and read several samples, and then buy the story they like best. This is a tremendous opportunity for writers. Are you using it?

Reader's Choice
I like ebooks because I can download several samples, try them all, then pick the one I enjoy most.

         - Rayne Hall

DO YOU HAVE SAMPLING DISABLED?

Most bookselling sites (such as Amazon) make the quarter or so of every book available as a free sample, but others (such as Smashwords) allow you to choose.

Don't refuse to give a free sample, thinking that that will force the reader to buy your book. She'll make her choice among the books which offer samples.

Here's an example from my own experience about how this works from a book buyer's perspective. I wanted to buy a cookery book with slow-cooker recipes. Finding several books on Smashwords, I wanted to take a peek inside to see if the recipes were simple enough for an unskilled cook like me. To my astonishment, several had disabled the sampling, so I had no idea whether those recipes were the sort I wanted. I downloaded samples of the three remaining ones, compared them, and bought the one which suited me best.

Suggested Action:

If you've disabled sampling, enable it right now.

IS YOUR SAMPLE TOO SHORT?

Although most sites set the length of the sample (e.g. 30% of the book), some sites allow the publisher to select 10%, 20%, 30% or 50%.

Select the biggest sample the site allows. The further the reader gets into the story, the more her desire to read on will grow. After reading one chapter, she can still leave and forget about it, but after reading half the book, she must find out what happens next.

Being stingy with the sample means the readers can't get hooked.

Suggested Action:

If your sample options are set to a low percentage, change it now. For a novel, I recommend 50%. For a short story collection, give at least one complete story. For a non-fiction book, I suggest two chapters.

DOES YOUR SAMPLE CONTAIN CLUTTER?

Readers who download the sample want to get a taste of

the story inside.

But too many sample pages show everything but story! They contain copyright notices, two blank pages, title and author, the publication date and publisher's location, legal disclaimers, acknowledgements, grateful thanks to the husband for providing tea and the cat for providing cuddles, dedications to people the reader has no interest in, a biography of the author, lists of other books by the author, reviews showing what other people think of the book, forewords by other writers—then "Like this book? Click here to buy it!"

Extensive front matter renders the sample pages useless. What a waste of a powerful marketing tool!

Suggested Actions:

Delete all the blank pages.

Combine all the small necessary stuff—copyright notices, publication dates, legal disclaimers—on a single page.

Move the acknowledgements, dedication, author bio, historical background and so on to the end of the book. In print books, they've customarily been part of the front matter, but ebooks don't need to follow this convention.

Remove the reviews. The reader has downloaded the sample because she wants to form her own opinion of your writing. (Put them to use elsewhere, perhaps on your website.)

CHAPTER 4: LINK DETOURS

Each time there's a link to click, most people won't click it. Their interest may be roused by your promotion, advertisement, guest post or interview—but when it comes to clicking, many just won't.

Some will. But if that URL leads to another page which then requires them to click again, they forget they ever had an interest in the book.

At each stop, you lose potential buyers. Estimates vary— some experts say the loss is 60%, some put it as high as 99%—but whatever the actual percentage, you can't afford it.

Once you have stirred the interest of potential readers, you need to direct them to where they can buy the book, with few or no stops in between. Don't direct them to a book trailer, your website or a landing page. Take them to the book.

To illustrate this, let's say you've written a Facebook post with a link to the Amazon page where they can buy the book, and 1,000 people click the link. After reading the blurb and maybe the sample, 10% decide to buy the book. That's 100 sales.

But if you send people from the Facebook post to a landing page where they find links to sites where they can buy the book, of the 1,000 people arrive at your landing site, 90% won't bother clicking on. Only 100 click through to Amazon, and if 10% of them decide to buy, that's 10 sales.

See the difference?

You can multiply your sales by removing the in-between steps.

DO YOU NEED A LANDING PAGE?

If you sell your book on different sites—Amazon, Barnes & Noble, Apple iBooks, Smashwords and others—each site has a different URL. Often, there isn't the room to list them all, especially not in tweets which limit the content to 140 characters.

That's why it can be useful to have a 'landing page' with links to all the sites where the book is sold. Is this a good idea? Maybe, maybe not. Bear in mind that many people won't click to the next step. They may reach your landing page, but not your book. You may lose most of your potential sales.

Suggested Actions:

If you have a landing page, don't delete it, but use it less.

Where the space allows, give the URLs to the three main sites selling the book.

If space is tight, choose the site where the majority of readers are likely to buy the book. Often this is Amazon, although for your books it could be a different retailer.

Use link shorteners to create abbreviated URLs. These enable you to put two or three links into a small space.

Experiment to see if this increases your sales. If not, you can always return to using the landing page.

DO THE DETOURS SAP PATIENCE?

Worse than landing sites are places which require the visitor to spend time. Book trailers are notorious for this. The viewer arrives, interested in the book, but then she has to watch several minutes of a boring advertising video. She probably won't watch it to the end—and she won't look for the book either.

Every second you delay the visitor lessens their interest in the book. It would have to be an unusually good trailer to maintain interest, and a miraculous one to make an already interested reader more interested.

Book trailers have their uses—but not as stopovers for readers whose interest is already whetted.

Suggested Actions:

Direct readers to the place where they can download the sample and click 'buy now'.

When creating trailers (and other promotional materials) keep them short and interesting. The shorter they are, the more likely the viewer will still be interested at the end.

DID YOU FORGET INTERNATIONAL READERS?

Some bookselling sites are accessible only to customers in certain countries. Amazon, for example, has separate businesses for the USA, UK, Canada, Australia, Brazil, Japan, India, Germany, France, Italy and Spain, and each has a different URL. Listing them all would be tedious. But if you list only one, you're excluding readers worldwide.

When you use your Amazon.com URL, readers outside the USA can click the link and see the book, but it would cost them a fortune in postage to buy the print book, and they can't buy the ebook at all. This is frustrating for them—and a frustrated viewer is not in the mood to buy. Even if they're still interested in the book, they have to click at least twice more to get to it. With each click, more of them fall by the wayside.

Suggested Action:

Use a universal link shortener that opens the Amazon page in the viewer's regional Amazon. Althou_ Amazon doesn't offer such URLs, some independent sites do, and it costs you nothing. The service providers may receive a small commission from Amazon for every sale. Try booklinker.net.

MISTAKES I MADE AND LEARNT FROM

I spent a lot of time creating trailers for my books, and then I tweeted to promote them. People praised the trailers (which were better than average) but didn't click to buy the books. I stopped tweeting about the trailers and tweeted about the books instead. Sales rose.

CHAPTER 5: KNOW YOUR READER

Many indie authors obsess about search engine optimisation, meta tags, Klout ranking, advertising, Google mentions, social media follower numbers and such—and forget what really matters: the reader.

Spend time learning about the people who read (or might read) your books, find out what they pay attention to, then go and engage them.

ARE YOUR READERS A GENERIC MASS?

Every book appeals to a different kind of person. What kind of person likes your kind of book? Who are the people for whom you have written it? If you reply, "My book is for everyone, men and women, any age, whatever their education and income, everywhere in the world," your marketing efforts are doomed.

If you can identify the typical reader—the kind of person who is most likely to love your book—you can sell far more books with far less work.

Suggested Action:

Define your target audience as tightly as possible. Examples:

• "Girls aged 14-17 who like everything to do with vampires, spend a lot of time watching DVDs and chatting on Facebook about boys, fashion and film stars."

• "Male geeks age 25-45 with a passion for electronic gadgets who want to be the first to own a new app. They watch science fiction movies, collect DVDs in boxed sets, and hang out with other geeks in online communities."

- "Parents of young children who are on a tight budget. They enjoy camping, do a lot of DIY, are always interested in saving money. Involved in their local community, use the internet only for shopping on eBay."

- "College-educated women age 40-60 who have a stressful life and crave romance. They care about health, fitness and pets, and are social media savvy."

DO YOU TARGET THE WRONG PEOPLE?

Many writers promote their books in the communities where they feel comfortable, instead of going out to meet real readers. Often, they promote their novels to other writers instead of to readers. They announce their book launch in online writers groups, keep a mailing list which consists of other writers, blog about how to write, and advertise on websites devoted to writers.

The real target audience never finds out about the book.

Suggested Action:

Go to places where your typical readers hang out, whether that's online or face to face, and connect with them. (More about this in Chapter 6.)

DO YOU PROMOTE IN THE WRONG PLACE?

Writers often spend much time and money advertising on websites which their readers never visit, promoting in newsletters to which their readers don't subscribe, and engineering mentions in social media where their readers don't hang out.

They pay to advertise their steamy romance on a website devoted to book marketing, their YA paranormal in a newsletter for aspiring writers, and their 'computer skills for absolute beginners' guide on Facebook.

Advertising in places where your typical reader doesn't go is money down the drain.

Suggested Action:

Focus your next advertising campaign on places where your typical reader actually spends time. (Be sceptical when advertising salespeople claim that masses of eager readers visit their website.)

MISTAKES I MADE AND LEARNT FROM

My background in magazine publishing protected me from wasting money on advertising which didn't reach the target audience—but it didn't stop me from wasting time.

In my early days as a professional writer, I had good contacts with the local newspapers, and knew exactly what kind of press releases would hook their journalists' interest. They frequently interviewed and featured me, especially when they needed material to fill the next week's paper. I got a lot of write-ups.

But it did this sell books? Nope.

Local newspaper readers would have been interested in novels set in their home town, or in job hunting guides for the local area. They were not keen buyers of historical novels set in foreign countries, or specialist books such as *How To Get A Job in Germany* and *Living & Working in China.*

All the time I spent crafting press releases was wasted. I should have written books and articles instead

CHAPTER 6: TARGETING VS SCATTERSHOT

If you promote your book to the general public, it takes a huge amount of effort and money to get a tiny result.

Promote your book to your target audience, and you get bigger results for a fraction of the work and cost.

ARE YOU SCATTERING YOUR RESOURCES?

Promoting your book is like sowing seeds. Some will sprout, some won't. Although some of it is down to luck, most is due to planning.

A gardener who sows his seeds on carefully selected fertile soil gets lush growth and can reap a fine harvest. But some gardeners are too lazy to study the soil and select the right spot. Instead, they scatter their seeds randomly, so that most fall on barren rock or asphalt where the plants have no chance.

Many new indie authors are like these lazy gardeners. They invest time and money in the seeds—and then toss them at random. What a waste!

Examples of scattershot promotions: advertising in mainstream magazines and on general interest websites, sending tweets from an account that doesn't have a targeted platform, bumper stickers on cars, radio commercials. Any of these may now and then accidentally reach a real reader—maybe one in 5,000. The other 4,999 are wasted. Can you afford the waste?

Suggested Actions:

Plan your next promotional activity so it reaches mostly the typical readers you've identified in Chapter 5.

Next time you pay for advertising, select a medium that reaches your specific audience. For example, advertise your horror novel in a horror magazine, and your historical romance on a historical romance website.

MISTAKES I MADE AND LEARNT FROM

Years ago when I still wrote for traditional publishers, my publisher's publicist arranged radio interviews for me. My books were non-fiction—*How To Get A Job In Germany, Living & Working In Germany, Living & Working in China,* and the like. Whenever something newsworthy happened in Germany or China, radio stations liked to have live interviews related to that country, and the publicist made use of that. I thought it was great—the BBC invited me as an expert guest, which meant I was a famous author!

In those days, radio interviews were involved. I had to spend several hours travelling to the studio, then sit in a glass cubicle with big headphones on my head, listening to music and waiting for the interviewer to ask a few questions every half hour or so. Each interview yielded maybe twenty minutes airtime, but required me to give up at least a day. I thought it was worth it, was delighted whenever the publicist arranged another interview, and complied happily.

In retrospect, I realise that it was a waste. Sure, the interview was broadcast to thousands of people. But how many of them were at that time interested in moving to Germany, and looking to buy a book about it? Very few indeed.

Frankly, I would have achieved more by staying at home and writing a chapter for the next book.

CHAPTER 7: PERMISSION VS INTRUSION

Most advertising is unwelcome. It intrudes where it's not wanted, disturbs the peaceful silence to blare its message, jolts people from whatever they were doing to get their attention. Examples: television commercials disrupting films, pop-up ads blocking out the web page we're reading. This is called Intrusion Marketing (or Disruption Marketing). At best, it gets ignored because people have become used to tuning out the irritating intrusions. When the commercials start, people mute the television, or leave their armchairs and make a cup of tea. At worst, it rouses anger. People remember the brand that disrupted their pleasure with annoyance or even nurture a rage against it.

Other advertising is welcome. People have agreed in advance to receive it because they are interested. Example: a newsletter people choose to subscribe to, or a mail order catalogue they request. This is called Permission Marketing. At worst, it gets ignored because people receive more than they can take in. At best, it is studied with keen interest, because the recipients genuinely want to find out about this.

Permission Marketing wins customers. Intrusion Marketing drives them away.

ARE YOU A SOCIAL MEDIA PEST?

Promote your book in the social media, but the line between Permission Marketing and Disruption Marketing is a fine one here. Make sure you understand the netiquette of the social network you are using.

Let's take Twitter as an example. By following you, people give you permission to post promotional tweets to their timeline. So go ahead and tweet about your book on special offer. Your followers may or may not read those tweets.

However, they have not given you permission to address your promotional message to them individually so it appears in their Direct Messaging box or their Notifications. If you do that, they'll get annoyed. They'll unfollow you, and may block you so you can't contact them ever again, and they may report you to Twitter so your account may get suspended.

Suggested Actions:

If you're currently using Intrusion Marketing in your social media network, stop it at once before you raise any more hackles.

Then send promotional messages through the accepted channels.

ARE YOU AN EMAIL FIEND?

Email is an inexpensive way to reach people—but you need their permission.

Many authors have great success with email lists. They invite their fans and other interested people to subscribe to a newsletter, and email them once a month or so with entertaining, informative content and book promotions. But you need to build an opt-in mailing list, and building one takes time.

Don't simply email everyone in your address book, or all the people you ever corresponded with, or harvest addresses from an online community. This is spam, and it may get your email account suspended. It will also ruin friendships and damage your reputation.

Suggested Actions:

If you've been spamming people with email, stop it at once before you do further harm to your reputation.

Build an opt-in email list. Since this takes time to grow, consider making it a joint project with other authors of your genre who write for the same target audience. At the end of each book, invite readers to subscribe.

DO YOU DISRUPT READERS?

When people visit your (or someone else's) website or blog to read what's there, they expect to see advertisements in the sidebars, and put up with them. But if they get flashing or noisy ads, or pop-ups blocking their view so they can't read on, they get angry. Angry readers won't buy your book.

Suggested Action:

If it's within your control, disable any flashing, noisy, or pop-up adverts immediately. Otherwise, cancel or don't renew the contracts, or ask to change them to a less intrusive style.

WEBSITE, BLOG, ADVERTISING

Visitors to your blog don't mind seeing your book covers in the sidebar while they read an interesting article. But when a pop-up advert flashes over the text so they can't read on, they get annoyed. Annoyed readers won't be interested in what the adverts says, and they won't want to spend money to read the book that caused the nuisance.

Forcing viewers' attention drives them away from your book.

Suggested Action:

Next time you advertise—whether it's on your own blog and website, or by paying for an advertisement somewhere else—avoid being a nuisance. Choose advertisements which attract, not annoy.

DO ONLINE GROUPS HATE YOUR NAME?

Having identified their target audience, writers often join online communities devoted to reading, to the fiction genre or the topic they write about. This is an excellent strategy—if you interact with the members in a helpful, entertaining, pleasant way.

Unfortunately, many writers use online groups to dump their promotions on the members. They post about their book, the trailers, the special offers. Readers' communities hate indie authors who do that. You'll definitely become unpopular fast, and members will recognise your name as a nuisance.

The moderators may ban you from their groups. By posting unwelcome promotions in online communities, you destroy your reputation, create bad feelings about your books, and ruin what might have been your best platform.

Suggested Actions:

Stop posting promotions in online communities.

Post interesting messages related to the topics of your books. If your posts about vampires are fascinating, members will soon associate your name with interesting vampire stuff—and buy your vampire novels.

Read other members' posts and comment on them, especially if they're related to your topic. People notice the people who notice them, and will reciprocate your interest.

CHAPTER 8: BURIED IN CEMETERIES

Many websites promise 'exposure' for payment. They sell you advertising (often called 'sponsorship' or 'feature') in return for space.

But the spaces on these sites are like graves on a cemetery—row after row after row of them, of no interest to anyone except the kin who placed them there, boring, ignored, dead.

Readers in search of their next book either go to a bookshop—brick or online—or a place with great articles about books and insightful book reviews. They don't visit ad cemeteries.

By promoting your book on cemetery sites, you gain nothing. You are throwing your money away.

IS YOUR PROMOTION BURIED IN A GRAVEYARD?

How to recognise cemetery sites:

* They display little or nothing other than advertisements and promotions.

* There's nothing on the site that would entice readers to spend time.

* Their declared purpose is 'to create exposure for writers' (instead of 'to provide information/entertainment for readers').

* The names are often a giveaway. Names like 'Writers' Promotion Paradise' and 'Author Exposure Buzz' are a clue that they're not serving readers, just milking authors.

* They have few followers/subscribers/visitors other than the authors who look at their own ads.

* If they claim large numbers of visitors, these are often faked. It's possible to buy automated visits to manipulate hit statistics and make a website seem popular. ('10,000 website views for only $49!')

Some websites have genuine interesting content which attracts readers—but your advertisement won't be on those pages. Instead, it gets dumped on a separate page which contains nothing but ads.

Suggested Actions:

If you've paid for the advertising campaign, it's too late to change it. Write it off as a loss, and start planning how to spend your next budget.

Save money by simply not advertising on those sites at all.

Advertise only on sites which are of interest to real readers, especially your target audience. (See Chapter 5.)

If you can afford it, place advertisements on the pages where the real content is (but this tends to be expensive).

DO YOUR PROMOTIONS LAND ON PROMO-DUMPING BLOGS?

Guest posts and excerpts on other people's popular blogs can be a great way to get your book noticed—but it depends on the quality of the blog.

Many people start a blog with best intentions, then don't have the time to write interesting posts so they fill it with ready-made material. But sourcing a constant supply of quality guest posts takes either time or money, so they hook up with book blog tour organisers. From them, they get an unlimited supply of fodder—bland promotions which they can just upload to their blog, no work required. Now the blog has nothing but promo after promo after promo (blurbs, excerpts, author interviews, cover reveals)—and nobody pays any attention.

Getting your books featured on those blogs has no benefit at all.

Suggested Actions:

Having your book featured on a promo-dumping blog doesn't do any harm, so don't stress about it. But if you've paid for the privilege (and blog tour organisers charge authors)—ouch!

Next time you pay for a book blog tour, compare several organisers. Investigate the blogs they supply. If those contain only promotional posts, choose a different one.

IS YOUR AD SHOVED INTO THE MAGAZINE'S IGNORED SECTION?

With printed magazines, the location of the advertisement matters more than anything else. Ads on the back cover and next to fascinating feature articles on the first pages get seen a lot, while those on the back pages gain little attention. Many magazines have a section at the end containing little or nothing but advertisements. Hardly any readers even glance at those parts.

Suggested Actions:

If you can afford it, put your advertisement in a prime location next to a topic-relevant editorial article—but be warned, those are very expensive.

If your budget doesn't stretch to that, don't advertise there at all. Save the money.

Only two people can say if a book is 'good enough' - the author and the reader. Gatekeepers are not needed.

- Rayne Hall

MISTAKES I MADE AND LEARNT FROM

I shudder when I think of all the money I spent on advertising during my first two years as an indie author of ebooks. I joined a lot of promotion programmes for authors to benefit from the exposure, until I realised that those sites were visited not by readers, but by other authors who went there to promote their own books.

Email newsletters targeted at readers of specific genres brought slightly better results. Advertising in those sometimes—not always—paid for itself. But the results were short-lived. I also grew fed-up with the newsletter owners telling me that my books were not good enough to be featured. Why should I jump through hoops, pay money and endure humiliation on top of that, when the results were negligible at best and often non-existent?

CHAPTER 9: SOCIAL MEDIA

Every social media message is a mini sample of your writing. If what you write is amusing, exciting or informative, your followers want to read more of the same... and that's when they buy your book.

Surprisingly few writers realise this. They churn out boring social media posts, mostly promotions of the kind that make readers yawn. The internet is already deluged with author interviews, novel excerpts, cover reveals, and announcements that books are reduced or free. The average reader sees hundreds of those every day and pays zero attention.

Some authors are smart. They post interesting stuff that's fun to read. If an author can write interesting tweets and Facebook posts, readers conclude that he can write interesting books, so they go and have a look.

What are your social media posts like? Do they convince your reader that you can entertain them?

DO YOUR BORE YOUR AUDIENCE?

Take a critical look at what you have sent from your social media accounts. Are these lively, funny, entertaining pieces which are a joy to read? Or is it mostly about your book, the same boring stream of 'buy my book' noise that thousands of other writers make?

Are your social media followers/friends/fans genuine people who read your posts? Or have they only subscribed to your feed so that you subscribe to theirs? Do they actually take note of what you say, discuss it, laugh about it, think about it for the rest of the day?

Suggested Actions:

Stop thinking of social media as a channel for promotions. View them as a way to win readers.

Reduce the frequency of promo posts. They're not getting noticed, so cutting down on them won't cause a loss.

Create interesting posts—not about your book. At this stage, many authors groan and say they don't know what to write about. Hey, wake up: you're a writer. Surely you can come up with something!

Other businesses need to hire writers to write their social media posts for them. You have the creativity and word skills to do it yourself.

Write about topics related to your book's content. If you're a paranormal romance author, write about vampire movies and werewolf lore. If your genre is historical fiction, post little-known quirky facts of that period.

As a fiction writer, seek to entertain your audience. If your posts are entertaining, the readers who enjoy them will seek out your books.

As a non-fiction writer, give helpful information. The author of books on thrifty household management can post tips how to save money on heating bills and how to grow vegetables from scraps.

You can still post promotional messages announcing that your novel is free next week or that you the latest book has been published today—but sparingly. The smaller the ratio of promotions, the more attention they will get.

HAVE YOU AUTOMATED YOUR SOCIAL MEDIA?

Managing a social media account takes time—more time than you can or want to spend. Many writers think they can cheat by automating their accounts. They use apps to send automated "thanks for following me" messages, to send out promotional posts several times a day, to fake their presence by automatically favouriting and sharing other people's posts.

But it doesn't help. Automation is a sure way to drive your real audience away. All you're left with is followers who don't read your messages, because they, too, have automated their accounts. Twitter and other social networks are full of people who automatically tweet, retweet and favourite one another's posts without ever looking at them. It's a fake world of robots interacting with robots.

Let's take Twitter as an example. Many indie authors think that by tweeting about their book, they can sell books. When this doesn't bring the desired results, they do it even more. They use a programme to automatically tweet promos every twenty minutes. Of course, this bores genuine followers, who stop paying attention. Frustrated by the lack of results, the authors conclude that they must promote even more. They join retweet cartels (which call themselves 'tweet teams') in which every member retweets every other member's tweets. The result is a mass of promo tweets advertising both their own and other people's books.

Bombarded with 1000 promotional tweets a day, the last genuine followers leave. All the author is left with is followers whose automated accounts are as fake as their own.

The author may be puzzled: their Klout ranking is going up, their Retweet rank is superb, their tweets are among the most favourited—so why does their book not sell?

When someone points out the futility of it all, they often whine, "But I need to create a buzz!" They don't want to believe that all this fake activity is of no use at all.

"Some people gain time by automating their Twitter accounts. I gain attention by being real."
– Rayne Hall

Suggested Actions:

Stop all automation at once. Auto-greet, auto-thanks, auto-follow, auto-retweet, auto-share, auto-like, auto-favourite—just cease.

You can continue to schedule posts (typing up several in advance, and schedule them to go out a few hours or days apart) but resist the temptation to fill the queues with promotional messages.

Get out of any like-swapping and auto-retweeting cartels. Once you stop doing it, you'll of course experience a drop in resharing rates. Keep in mind that those are pointless reshares, and forgoing them is no loss. Indeed, once you stop reposting other people's junk, your decluttered stream will become much more attractive.

Share only interesting posts—the kind your readers want to read. Focus on making it worthwhile for your followers to read what you share.

Now write real posts—entertaining, helpful ones.

Use social networks the way they are meant to be used—for socialising. Interact with your followers, chat with them, read their posts, ask questions, discuss issues. Notice them, and they will notice you.

Simply by being genuine, you'll soon stand out. Followers will flock to you because you're real.

If you reckon that you can't possibly have the time to write genuine posts and interact on all social networks, you're right. Pick one social network—the one you're most comfortable with and where many of your prospective readers hang out—and build a genuine platform there. Forget the others. One social network with a genuine platform is worth more than a dozen social networks with automated accounts.

If you have hired a social media manager, check what they're doing. If their strategy consists of churning the same dull promotions over and over and swapping fake likes, fire them. Then hire someone whose strategy is based on interaction and authenticity.

MISTAKES I MADE AND LEARNT FROM

For a short time, I got infected by the retweet-obsession. I retweeted other authors' tweets like crazy, even used an auto-retweeting service, so that they would retweet mine. It did not take me long to realise that this was driving my followers away. They stopped reading my tweets as well as my retweets. When I cancelled all the automation, new followers flocked to my account. These were real people, not other automated accounts. They read my tweets, chatted with me—and bought my books.

CHAPTER 10: WEBSITES, BLOGS AND OTHER TIME SINKS

You need an internet presence, a way for publishers, journalists and fans to contact you. But you may not need as much as you think.

Many writers keep a blog, maintain a website, create book trailers and curate online communities. These can be useful—but often they do more harm than good. As promotional tools, they are often worthless.

To get those sites noticed, you need to promote them. Would it not be better to promote your book?

DO YOU SPEND YOUR WRITING TIME BLOGGING?

You have to take time to write a blog, and where do you take the time from? It's the time you would otherwise spend writing books.

What is more likely to sell books? Keeping a blog, or having a list of great published books for sale?

Although there may be exceptions, for most authors it's more useful to invest their time in writing more books and revising them to a high standard. Unless your blog has a huge audience of eager engaged readers, and unless data shows that your blog drives sales, take drastic measures.

Suggested Actions:

If your blog has few followers, or only half-hearted ones who seldom bother to read the posts, if you struggle to find the time and quality content, if your recent posts contained apologies for not posting more and promises to do better in

RAYNE HALL

the future, or if it has degenerated into a dull promo dump, simply stop blogging. Shedding the stress will be such a relief!

If you keep several blogs, close all but the one which genuinely reaches your book's target audience. For an author of vampire romance, the vampire blog may be worth maintaining, but the writing and gardening blogs can be closed.

If blogging genuinely helps your book's sales, but it devours too much of your time, find partners with whom to share it. A shared blog takes a fraction of the time, and pulls in more followers. Select partners who write for the same target audience, who you know to be pleasant and reliable, and who share your values.

If you write great blog posts and enjoy creating them, but find the regular commitment draining and your blog doesn't reach the big audience it deserves, close your blog. Instead, write guest posts on other people's blogs. This way, you can tap into their ready-made audiences, which gives you a much better reach. You don't need to produce regularly. You can even recycle your old blog posts and share them again and again on different blogs.

IS YOUR WEBSITE OUT OF DATE?

Websites can be useful, but only if they are well-maintained. A website announcing "New book coming in December 2012" puts visitors off. It can even undermine the author's credibility, especially with non-fiction.

Many writers design complex websites which require intense upkeep. A simple website is almost always better than a complex one.

And sometimes, no website at all is best.

46

Suggested Actions:

If you spend much time maintaining your website or if it contains out-of-date information because you haven't got round to updating it, reduce the stress. Simplify your website. Delete the interactive forums, the news page and anything requiring your moderation or input. Give up the direct sales shop (unless it makes a lot of money, of course) and let Amazon and other retailers sell the book for you.

Your website needs a list of your currently published books (use the phrase 'recent books include', so it won't matter if you don't immediately get around to adding the latest title), an author bio (phrased so that it needs updating only every five years or so), links to where readers can buy your books (e.g. Amazon and Barnes & Noble—keep those links up to date), and a means of contacting you. Everything else can go.

Consider shutting your website down. You need a web presence of some kind where publishers and readers can find and contact you, but it doesn't need to be your own website. Use your blog, or share a website with several other writers of your genre.

ONLINE COMMUNITIES

Curating communities can be stimulating and rewarding—but it's not a tool to increase sales.

The time required to run a group, forum or community is enormous. You need to provide constant stimulating input, police behaviour, arbitrate disputes, deter promo dumpers, deal with troublemakers, solve technical glitches and more, to keep it flourishing. View it as a good deed, a way of giving back to the community and earning positive karma—because it's not an effective strategy for selling books.

An online fan club won't attract many members until you're famous, and in any other group, members will resent it when you target them with promotions.

Suggested Actions:

Close any groups that are ailing. If members don't post, if spammers have invaded or if the community has degenerated into flame wars, just shut it down.

If the group is thriving but taking up too much of your time, resign the leadership. Hand the mantle over to an eager member who has been participating actively for a long time. You can stay on as an ordinary member.

Consider joining several groups as a member instead of running your own. Select the kind of communities where your typical prospective readers hang out, and become a valued contributor.

MISTAKES I MADE AND LEARNT FROM

I used to participate in dozens of online groups, most of which were of no use to me whatsoever. I spent time crafting thoughtful posts which gained little attention or even earned derision from trolls, and I put much time and energy into leading writers' groups, giving my precious energy to people who didn't even appreciate it. Nowadays I'm ruthless. I lead a few online writing groups— such as the Professional Authors Group and Rayne's Writers' Research Club—and am a member of a few which don't require much time. I still give my time and energy generously, but I no longer throw it away.

CHAPTER 11: STOP OBSESSING OVER WHAT DOESN'T MATTER

Throwing themselves into the whirlpool of online promotions, writers imitate what other businesses do: they chase Google mentions, obsess about search engine optimisation (SEO) and strive to increase their ranking in social media popularity charts.

But none of these have much effect on book sales.

Readers looking for the next great book to buy don't say, "I'll buy this novel because it's listed at #6948 in the Goggle search engine for the keyword 'romance', whereas that one is only #7892."

They don't say, "This thriller looks exciting. I'll pop over to Klout to see what influencer ranking the author has before I decide."

The places where rankings and exposure matter are the sites selling books: Amazon, Barnes & Noble, iBooks, Smashwords and so on. That's where every improvement brings real gains.

Stop obsessing about the irrelevant and focus on what matters.

DO YOU OBSESS OVER SEO?

Search engine optimisation is useful for some businesses—but not for writers. Social media professionals and online service providers try to convince everyone that it's vital to have your name come up in a search above that of your competitors. But for us, that's nonsense.

Readers don't care what a book's or author's place in the Google, Ask, Bling or DuckDuckGo is. A higher ranking won't get you better known and it won't sell more books.

Suggested Actions:

Simply stop your quest for improved search engine ranking. Save the time and money and invest them in more useful measures.

The exception: if you're writing books on 'SEO for Professionals', then your credibility depends on your name and title featuring among the top search engine results.

ARE YOU CHASING PERCEIVED POPULARITY?

Many apps and services claim to measure your online popularity and success. Once you get sucked into this trap, it's easy to become addicted, trying to add another percentage point or credit to your 'success'.

But these services are so easy to manipulate that they're useless. All it takes is a few people agreeing to retweet and share one another's social media posts, and the participants' rankings will skyrocket, even if no real people read the posts. Another way is to open a dozen accounts in different names, and let them automatically retweet your tweets. Suddenly you get a high 'retweet rank' and are considered an 'influencer' on Klout. But these are just new clothes for the emperor, because it's all pretence and no substance.

Suggested Action:

Cancel the popularity-measuring services you've subscribed to. You'll find better ways to spend that money.

Stop the quest for retweets, likes, favourites, shares, K+ and such. Invest your time in more constructive activities. Beware: if you've been feeding your ego with popularity measurements for some time, the habit can be hard to break. You may get withdrawal symptoms like an addict.

HOW TO GET YOUR BOOK NOTICED WHERE IT MATTERS

Where your book is ranked on the book-selling sites (Amazon, Barnes& Noble etc.) really matters, because the bestselling books get more exposure which in turn leads to more sales.

Placing your book on a book site's bestseller list—even if it's only a sub-sub-genre bestseller list—can make all the difference. It's not about bragging rights ("I am a bestselling author") but because of the increased exposure on the site itself. Readers browsing for their next book of a specific kind often look at the current bestseller lists in their favourite genres.

If you can get your book into the top twenty of its sub-genre, it may soon ride an upward spiral.

The challenge lies in how to get that good ranking in the first place. The number of sales is the main factor, and your sales aren't glorious yet, or you wouldn't have bought this book.

However, there are several strategies worth pursuing. They take effort, but this is time worth spending.

Suggested Actions:

The key to getting your book into a bestseller list is choosing the right categories. Book-selling sites allow the indie-publishing author to choose several genres. Choose wisely.

Pick as many genres as the site permits. Some allow only

two, others up to seven. Most books straddle several sub-genres or even main genres.

Select appropriate genres. The genre tag raises reader expectations. If you label the book 'Romance', readers expect a love story with a happy ending, and leave nasty reviews if that's not what they get. If you put your Erotica novel into the Chicklit Category to circumvent the retailer's 18+ restriction, you get more exposure, but of the wrong kind; instead of attracting your target audience who like steamy fiction you reap angry responses from outraged buyers.

Opt for sub-sub-genres rather than main genres. If the choice is between 'Fantasy' and 'Epic Fantasy' pick the latter. Aim to make your book a big fish in a small pond.

Choose the smallest ponds available. Which category has the fewest books? Let's say your book is an Epic Fantasy based on the King Arthur myth. The Epic Fantasy category has thousands of books, the Arthurian Fantasy only two dozen. In this case, your novel is practically guaranteed a place in the Top 100 Arthurian Fantasy books, and if it's a great story and you promote it well, it could catapult into the Top 10.

Be aware that different countries have different category systems. This is especially noticeable on the different Amazon sites. When you upload the book, you get to choose only from the American system, and the best-fitting categories don't even show.

Moreover, Amazon's actual catalogue uses far more categories than are available for selection to authors. The publishing categories don't reflect the full range of sales categories, and you may not be able to pick the sub-categories for which your book would be a perfect fit and where there is almost no competition.

For example, sales for my book *13 British Horror Stories* increased once it was in the 'British and Irish Short Stories' category—but this was not an option available when I published the book.

How do you get into these categories? It takes time and persistence. Identify the categories in which your book belongs, then contact Amazon's KDP Support staff and ask them to move it there. You may reach a human person who carries out your request immediately. At other times you may run against a wall of automated replies and won't get anywhere.

To make matters more complicated, categories can differ between print books and ebooks, and they change as the retailers add new categories or restructure their system.

Books also get automatically put into categories, based on the keywords. For example, if you put your book into the category 'Western' and your keywords include 'love', the book is automatically added to the Western Romance category. Choose your keywords wisely!

Sometimes, I'm bewildered by the categories my books end up in. My single-author story collections are bestsellers in 'Anthologies' (that is, multi-author books—and I swear I did not put them there), and one of my horror books was a bestseller in 'English-Language Children's Books' on the Italian Amazon.

Most retail and distribution sites (Amazon, Smashwords, Draft2Digital etc.) allow the publisher to provide several keywords. These help readers find the books they like. Use all the keywords you are allowed, be as specific as possible, and don't waste the allowances on repeating the title or genre categories.

As soon as one of your books has hit the Top 100 in a retailers' bestseller list, shift all your promotional efforts to that retailer and that book, to catapult it to the very top.

At certain times of the year, landing on a bestseller is easier than at others. When sales are generally low, a book needs to sell only a few dozen copies to get into the Top 10 of a small bestseller list. My book *Cutlass: Ten Tales of*

Pirates once got on a bestseller list although it had sold only nine copies that month. For most genres, this is during July and August. You may want to concentrate your promotional efforts on that period, aiming not for huge sales but for a place on a bestseller list. This gives the book exposure which will increase sales in subsequent weeks.

MISTAKES I MADE AND LEARNT FROM

For a while, I got caught up in the search engine optimisation frenzy. I tried to ensure that every website or blog post mentioning me got a high placement in the search engines. I even paid a service to manipulate the results. When someone googled 'Rayne Hall', the first ten results had to be about me! Whenever a search of 'Rayne Hall' yielded the website of the community hall of Rayne village among my profiles, and whenever there were more pictures of the Tampa Bay Storm Dancers than of my novel *Storm Dancer*, I worked obsessively to drive those off the first Google page.

Eventually I took a step back and asked myself what I was doing. Who cared whether all ten results on the first Google page were about me? What harm did the mention of a village hall do to my reputation or my sales? If anyone googled 'Storm Dancer', would seeing a cheerleading troupe put them off reading my book?

I had wasted a lot of time and energy, as well as quite a bit of money, on the futile pursuit of SEO.

CHAPTER 12: HOW TO GET REAL BOOK REVIEWS

Many readers check reviews before they buy a book. Reviews, especially on major book-selling sites such as Amazon, have become an important sales tool.

But first, you need to get them. In their pursuit of reviews, many authors shoot themselves in the foot.

DO YOU HAVE TOO FEW REVIEWS?

The first few reviews are the most difficult to get, and you need to use your initiative to bring them about.

Asking established book reviewers to read your book is a possibility, although they are inundated with requests. Their silences and rejections remind us of the days of traditional publishing when we submitted our manuscripts to agents and editors, with little hope of success.

Suggested Actions:

Ask the beta readers who critiqued your book before publication. They have already read it, know it well and probably like it (especially if you applied their suggestions).

At the end of your book, add a 'Dear Reader' section in which you say how much it would please you if they posted a review.

When fans contact you to say how much they enjoyed your book, ask if they would consider writing a review. Many are flattered to be asked.

In your social media, post messages: "Would anyone like to review my book [title] on Amazon? Free ebook for reviewers." Giving free books is legitimate, but don't offer anything else—no money, bribes, prize draws or gifts.

Be careful about paying review agencies. Some are cowboys, taking your money and never delivering reviews. Many others deal in fake reviews (see below).

DO NEGATIVE BOOK REVIEWS GET YOU DOWN?

Cheer up. Negative reviews can be good for sales!

A thoughtful review by a reader who explains what he disliked about the book may inspire others to buy it. A review complaining that a collection of horror stories is 'not gory enough' signals that this is the perfect book for readers who like subtle scares. If the review is negative because your romance novel 'lacks sex' it will make the book attractive to readers who prefer their romances chaste.

Daft reviews written by obvious idiots are good news, too. They encourage intelligent people to buy the book.

The only way to avoid getting negative book reviews is not to write books.

- Rayne Hall

Suggested Actions:

Rejoice in the negative reviews if you can. If that's difficult, then ignore them. If they really upset you to the point where you want to give up writing, then stop reading reviews.

For a laugh, head over to my guest blog post http://venturegalleries.com/blog/have-you-ever-received-any-negative-reviews-that-were-really-funny-most-authors-have/ where I've compiled the silliest negative book reviews I've received. They're bound to make you chuckle.

HAVE YOU RESPONDED TO REVIEWS?

You shouldn't. Don't argue with reviewers, or you'll lose your readers' respect. But don't respond to praise either.

Customer reviews are not for authors. They are for other customers. If an author meddles, he comes across as interfering, patronising or insecure.

Authors who responded to customer reviews found that as soon as they got involved, the reviews became more negative, scathing even.

Some trolls and cyber-bullies seek out indie authors purely to provoke them into fights. They use nasty personal attacks. Don't be tempted to defend yourself or your book, or to hit back at the aggressors. Your response motivates them to continue, and they'll attack your other books next. If you ignore them, they'll go away.

Customer reviews are not critique services to help the writer improve their work. The time for that is before publication.

Suggested Actions:

Stop replying to reviews. Delete any comments you have

already posted.

Put your email address at the end of the book, and invite readers to contact you.

ARE YOU PRESENTING FAKE REVIEWS?

When real reviews aren't forthcoming, many authors try to buy them. Indeed, there are plenty of places selling reviews. You can get ten guaranteed five-star reviews for $20, and if you pay more, they'll even be 'verified purchases'. Beware: these are fakes, even if they are advertised as 'genuine honest reviews'. The people who sell reviews are in it for the money. They churn out reviews without wasting time reading the book.

Don't be tempted.

Buying reviews is against the rules at Amazon and other sites. If you are found out (and you almost certainly will be), Amazon will delete the fake reviews—and you'll be on record as an author who tries to cheat.

You won't fool real readers either. The kind of reader who consults reviews before buying a book recognises fakes. They won't fall for the 'Absolutely unputdownable book! Best author since Shakespeare!' crap. Instead, they conclude that the book must be awful if the author stoops to fakes.

If readers do indeed fall for the cleverly constructed fakes, you may get a few sales—but then it backfires. The expectations raised by the reviews are not met. The angry readers return the book for a refund, and leave scathing reviews. When Amazon deletes the fake reviews, the scathing ones remain. You're left with nothing but two-star reviews by readers who explain why your book is so bad.

Suggested Actions:

Stop buying fake reviews at once.

Getting rid of the ones you already have is difficult. You need to contact the reviewers and ask them to delete their contributions. Many won't even respond to this request. If you've bought the reviews through an agency, contacting the individual reviewers is impossible.

You can ask the book retailing site to remove the fake reviews—but that means admitting that you have offended against the rules and cheated. Show contrition and promise not to do it again.

The other alternative is more drastic: unpublish the book and publish it again, starting with a clean slate.

HAVE YOU FALLEN INTO THE REVIEW SWAP TRAP?

Desperate to get reviews, some indie authors band together to review one another's books. It seems a neat solution—but it's a quagmire.

Either the reviewers are honest—which leads to hurt feelings when one doesn't love the other's book—or the reviewers put 'helping one another' above honesty, and pretend to love a book they disdain. They deliberately mislead the book-buying public by writing a glowing review, confidently expecting a five-star review in return. In consequence, readers come to mistrust book reviews, that particular author, and indie authors in general.

Review swaps are unethical, and against the rules of most review sites. By swapping reviews, you show disrespect for the most important people, the genuine book-buying reader. Is this the signal you want to send—that you're a cheat, and despise readers?

On big sites like Amazon, a whole community of reviewers have emerged, competitive and ferociously protecting the reviewing system. When they spot review swaps (and they're good at spotting them), they name and shame the authors. You'll look like a pathetic fool.

Suggested Actions:

Don't engage in review swaps. If you've already done it, stop before you damage your image further.

If you have only one or two swap reviews, hope that you'll soon get many reviews from genuine customers, so your swap reviews will no longer be noticed.

But if your book's review section is loaded with swap reviews, you need to take tough measures to distance yourself. Ask the authors you swapped to remove their reviews, while you delete yours.

Be prepared—not all will take this kindly. They have spent time composing a flattering review, and they count on your five-star rating to give their own book a fake glamour.

Point out that Amazon is enforcing the rules more strictly these days and that you don't want to be seen offending.

HAVE YOU DUMPED YOUR OWN PROMOS INTO BOOK REVIEWS?

Some authors abuse the review system by reviewing other people's books and inserting promos for their own. "If you like this kind of book, don't miss mine!"

They even recruit their friends to post reviews such as, "This book is crap. Read my mate's book instead, it's much better!"

One such review is enough to damage your image. The reader sees you as desperate, unethical, pathetic, untrustworthy—not someone they want to spend time with. If you have planted several such reviews on the internet, don't be surprised if readers avoid you because your very name smells bad.

Suggested Actions:

Delete any such reviews at once. Ask your friends to delete theirs, too—and you may have to be diplomatic in requesting them to undo the 'favour' you had asked them for. Hope that the people who read your pathetic 'reviews' have forgotten your name, and don't repeat your mistake.

Search the internet to see if your book and author name have already become an object of disdain among the reading community. If they have, the only way forward is to start with a clean slate. Unpublish the book, republish it with a new title, and use a different pen name.

MISTAKES I MADE AND LEARNT FROM

Soon after I took up indie publishing in earnest, I realised that my books needed customer reviews, but those weren't forthcoming. When other authors claimed to adore my novel and offered to review it if I reviewed theirs, I agreed eagerly. To my horror, those books were not very good. I told the authors that the review would be a negative one, and asked them if they wanted me to post it anyway.

Some responded with hurt, others with aggression. Some informed me that I was wrong not to like their book and demanded I read it again. One informed me that she was the vice-president of a romance writers group and therefore I was mistaken in finding fault with her work. One changed her own five-star review of *Storm Dancer* to a two-star one.

Another tried blackmail: unless I reviewed her novel with five stars, she would get all her friends to write scathing reviews of mine.

I no longer engage in review swaps.

In the early stages, I was so desperate to get reviews, that I purchased them. "Genuine honest Amazon review—$5" the advertisements promised. The resulting reviews were neither genuine nor honest. The 'reviewers' didn't read the book. They simply copied some phrases from the blurb and from other people's reviews, added hyperbolic praise, and posted it on Amazon.

Some even posted identical reviews for several books by different authors.

The most blatant fake went like this: "This novel kept me awake all night. I loved the characters! This author will be remembered as one of the literary greats along with Charles Dickens and Jane Austen." It was not a novel, but a non-fiction book.

I was so embarrassed by these obvious fakes! Fortunately, Amazon cracked down on fake reviews and deleted them all. The reviews you see now are genuine, and there's no shortage of them.

However, I've learnt my lesson: people who write paid reviews are in it for the money, and they want to earn a lot of money fast. Why would they waste hours reading a book if they can churn out a review in five minutes?

CHAPTER 13: END-MATTER EXCERPTS

A book excerpt at the end of a similar book is the most effective tool. Surprisingly, many indie authors don't use it.

HAVE YOU MISSED THIS TRICK?

When a reader has finished reading a book, he's ready to read another. The fact that he's reached the end of the book means he probably enjoyed it, and is open to something similar. If your book's end-matter contains the beginning of a similar book, he'll read it, and if he likes it, he'll get hooked and want to read now. This leads to many sales for that book.

You'll see the amazing effect in the online retailers' 'Customers Who Bought This Also Bought' feature.

No other promotional tool reaches the target audience (readers who love this kind of book and are on the brink of buying another one) as effectively as excerpts in the end-matter. With ebooks, this wonderful tool costs you nothing.

Suggested Actions:

If you have several books in the same genre, put the first couple of chapters of each in the end-matter of another. If it's a serial, include the beginning of the next volume.

The aim is not to provide a sample of your writing style, but to make the reader read on and hook him on the new story.

If you haven't published another similar book yet, swap excerpts with another author whose books are similar to yours. The more similar, the better. If your book is a YA Vampire Romance, then another author's YA Vampire

Romance is best, though a YA Werewolf Romance is almost as good. By including another author's excerpt, you're endorsing that book, so make sure it's of high quality. Don't accept anything substandard, or it will reflect badly on you.

If you plan to publish more books of the same genre but they are not ready yet, arrange a temporary excerpt swap with another author. Suggest that you swap excerpts for one year; when that period is over, you can either renew the agreement or drop it.

If you like, you can include excerpts of two or three books, although the individual effectiveness is lower.

Caution: don't overdo the excerpts. If the excerpts take up more space in your book than the main content, readers get angry.

With print books, you may have to be careful. Long excerpts add to the number of pages, which increases the printing cost. You may decide to use shorter excerpts in the paperback than in the ebook.

Reader's Choice:
I care little if a book is traditionally or indie published. I just want a good read.

- Rayne Hall

MISTAKES I MADE AND LEARNT FROM

When I started publishing my Writer's Craft books, I added excerpts of my fiction, hoping that some readers would fancy an epic fantasy novel. I should have added excerpts of my other Writer's Craft books.

Once I swapped endmatter excerpts with another writer who then unpublished her book without telling me. Readers who saw the excerpt and wanted to read the rest were left high and dry – and they blamed me.

CHAPTER 14: SHARED MARKETING

When you join forces with another indie author, you can halve your marketing workload and double your results—but only if you choose the right partner.

Here are some marketing endeavours suitable for sharing between authors:

- blog

- email newsletter

- website

- Facebook (or any other social media account)

- end-matter excerpts

ARE YOU STILL DOING IT ALONE?

When authors write for the same target audience and pool their followers/subscribers, they multiply their reach. They can take turns posting on Facebook, writing blog posts and contributing to the newsletter. In one swoop, they reduce their stress, gain time, and increase potential sales.

Alternatively, each writer can take responsibility for one social media network, build a quality platform there and promote the other writers' work along with her own. This way, you reach audiences who would not otherwise be aware of your book.

There's no way one writer alone can entertain audiences in several social media, keep a blog, write a newsletter and maintain a website on her own, and still have time to write and live a life. You may have tried shortcuts such as automating your Twitter and filling your blog with promotional posts, and found that instead of attracting potential readers, it drove them away.

Suggested Actions:

Find a partner (or several). She should be an author who writes in the same genre, and if possible the same sub-genre, so your target audience is the same.

Choose someone whom you know already, perhaps a writer who is a member of the same online genre writing group, and whom you've observed to be well-organised, pleasant and reliable. Don't take risks with strangers.

You can also form a group. Group blogs and shared newsletters work well. One of you acts as the coordinator. If your group has several projects (a newsletter, a blog and Facebook account, perhaps), then each member takes responsibility for one project.

If you enjoy reading a blog by a writer of your genre, ask her if she's interested in a partnership. She can only say no. Perhaps you can start by becoming a guest blogger, and if it works out, you can expand your role.

Perhaps there's a group blog which would be just right for you? Let them know you're interested if they ever have a vacancy. Until then, leave insightful comments.

For any shared promotion, draw up a written (emailed) agreement about who contributes what and when, and who is in charge for what. This prevents fights and frustrations.

Easier to arrange are mutual promotions in different media. If you have many followers on Twitter, while another has a popular Facebook page and a third has a vibrant account on Google+, each uses her platform to promote the others' books alongside her own.

DO YOU TARGET DIFFERENT AUDIENCES?

However pleasant it is to work with her, you are both wasting your resources. You may think it's a great idea to offer varied content to appeal to different types of reader—but the results are minuscule. Readers pay far more attention to a blog devoted to the kind of book they're passionate about, than one which deals with books in general.

Suggested Action:

If your partner does not write for the same audience, separate. Explain that you want to try a different promotion strategy, targeting your specific audience, so she doesn't think you're finding fault with her. She is probably as frustrated with the lack of results as you are, and will understand.

Don't just drop out of the arrangement. Give her plenty of notice so she can make other arrangements. Keep on good terms and continue to help each other with advice and moral support. Find a partner who has books published in the same genre as you.

If you belong to a mutual-promotion group or joint blog which doesn't reach your target audience, resign from it and seek one with a better fit. Tell your partners in advance that you intend to leave, and meet your existing commitments. Don't suddenly leave them in the lurch.

ARE YOU LINKED WITH AN AUTHOR WHO WRITES LOW QUALITY?

When you promote another author, you're endorsing her books. If they are substandard, not only does it reflect on your taste, but people will assume that your writing is as bad as that writer's.

This is applies especially to excerpt swaps in the book's end-matter.

Suggested Action

Terminate the arrangement, but try to do this without causing bad feelings and burning bridges. You may want to simply say that since the current promotions aren't yielding enough sales, you need to try something new.

ARE YOUR MARKETING PARTNERS NOT PULLING THEIR WEIGHT?

With collaborations, there's often one participant who doesn't meet her commitments, does perfunctory work, fails to keep promises, and misses deadlines. This causes stress for the others, who need to do that member's work as well as their own, and under enormous time pressure. Each time this member lets the readers down, it reflects badly on the whole group. The damage is substantial.

Suggested Action:

Be ruthless and get rid of that person. This can be done in a diplomatic way without hard feelings. Simply say that since she's obviously struggling to meet her commitments at the moment, you'll do it without her for a while to give her breathing space, and maybe she can join again in the future when her circumstances have changed. She'll probably react with relief, grateful to shed the stressful burden.

Then continue without her, and recruit a new partner you can count on.

MISTAKES I MADE AND LEARNT FROM

I agreed to promote other authors' books on Twitter, in return for them promoting mine on Facebook, LinkedIn and other social networks. While I kept my side of the bargain, they didn't, and I discovered this only months later.

Several times, I was part of a joint project (a website, a blog, a special event) where every participating author was to contribute an equal amount of work. I ended up doing almost all the work; the others contributed only promises and excuses. The projects fizzled out, and I had lost a lot of time. Nowadays, I would launch a new project only with authors I know to be dependable.

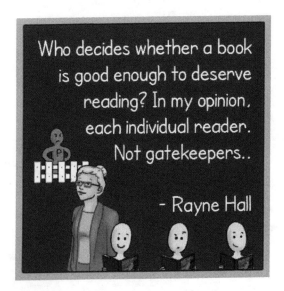

Who decides whether a book is good enough to deserve reading? In my opinion, each individual reader. Not gatekeepers..

- Rayne Hall

CHAPTER 15: ONCE-EFFECTIVE METHODS NO LONGER WORK

Books and blog posts tell of how certain authors had phenomenal success by using certain methods.

But when you use the methods, they don't work for you. Indeed, they no longer work for anyone.

In part this is because when thousands of people do the same thing, the effect dilutes, readers become bored, the promotion gets ignored.

The other reason is that circumstances change.

For example, making a book free for a few days was a powerful marketing technique in 2011. Readers snatched up the book while it was free, which catapulted it up in the Amazon bestseller charts, and the increased exposure continued to attract more sales. But Amazon's algorithms have changed repeatedly since then. Free downloads count for almost nothing, so they no longer lead to increased exposure. Moreover, readers are inundated with free books. With hundreds of thousands of free ebooks available, the offer of yet another free one doesn't set anyone's heart racing.

Authors who reveal how they achieved bestsellerdom a few years ago are telling the truth—but don't expect their recipe to work for you. Reader preferences, publishing practices, trends and algorithms change rapidly these days. By the time you copy someone else's success technique, it's already useless.

ARE YOU USING OUTDATED METHODS?

Impressed by a successful indie author's strategy, you're imitating what they did. But the phenomenal sales don't happen. You persevere, convinced that it's only a matter of time. It worked for that author, so it has to work for you, doesn't it? But all the money, time, effort and hope you put into it just drain away.

Suggested Actions:

By all means try the methods which worked for others. If they work for you, good—but if not, stop.

Use those authors' success stories as encouragement rather than as a blueprint. Let them inspire you to find your own route to success. Those authors experimented and found their own way. That's what you need to do.

When a new indie author hits your genre's bestseller lists, study their methods. They may work for you, too, but you have to be quick and act before everyone else uses the same approach.

Experiment. Try new things until you hit on a strategy which works.

DO YOU FAIL TO ADAPT?

Your books used to sell really well. You had a great promotion strategy and a bag of tricks which catapulted your books to the top every time. But now sales have dropped and you can't revive them, although you do exactly what you used to, and put even greater effort into it than before.

Suggested Action:

Face it—the market has changed, trends have changed, reader expectations have changed. You need to update your strategy. Give up the methods which once worked but no longer. Don't waste any more time and money pursuing them. Instead, experiment with new approaches. You obviously have the ability to develop effective strategies; use this skill again.

MISTAKES I MADE AND LEARNT FROM

After reading about the phenomenal success other authors enjoyed by making a book free for five days, I did it as well, not realising that the glory days of free books were already past. I achieved 16,000 downloads, and confidently expected sales to soar. They didn't.

I assumed that I had been doing it wrong, so I tried it again with another book. This time, I had only 11,000 downloads. The next yielded only 800.

But it had worked for that other author, so it had to work for me! I tried harder and harder. I promoted the free downloads on Twitter and Google+. I submitted like crazy to sites that promoted promotions. I paid a service that submitted my promotion to sites that promoted promotions. I paid for advertising.

But every time, the number of free downloads was smaller—and neither my Amazon sales ranking nor the number of book sales rose.

Eventually I faced the truth: with so many thousands of free books available, readers just aren't interested in yet another one. The freebie gluttons who download dozens of free books every week never get round to reading them.

I was wasting my time and my money on something that had worked in 2011, but no longer worked in 2013.

What relief that realisation was! I could save my time and money, stop ramming freebies down people's throats, and instead promote my books to real readers who were willing to pay for a good book.

I still give away some books free—but these are short stories I make perma-free, to hook new fans who will then buy my novels.

CHAPTER 16: DISTRIBUTION CHANNELS

In 20th century publishing, books went via publishers, distributors and bookshops to the reader. Now, most book sales happen online—and you choose the distribution channels.

DO YOU RELY ON YOUR OWN WEBSITE?

Some authors sell their books exclusively on their own website, or their own market trading stall.

This way, distributors like Amazon can't take a cut, and all the money goes to the author.

But very few readers visit an unknown author's website, and rarely will passers-by stop at a stall to view a book. The promotion required to get anyone's attention is immense, and sales are near zero.

Suggested Actions:

Upload your book on Amazon, Barnes & Noble, Apple etc., where thousands of eager readers go every day looking to buy books like yours. Let the big guys do the bulk of the marketing for you. The percentage they take of the income is deserved.

If you feel daunted by the prospect of handling several sales channels at once, publish your book with Smashwords or Draft2Digital and let them distribute it to the major channels.

You can keep the sales option on your own website if it yields any sales. If not, close it.

ARE YOU RELYING ON A SINGLE CHANNEL?

Some book retailers want to get a monopoly on your book. They want to be the only ones who have it in their catalogue. Amazon, for example, constantly lures you into surrendering your independence and making the book exclusive to Amazon by enrolling it in KDP Select. If you agree to this, you can't sell your ebook anywhere else.

You're missing out on potential sales on Barnes & Noble, Apple and other places—and who knows, your book might be a top bestseller there!

Suggested Action:

If you've committed your book to Amazon's KDP Select (or another retailer's monopoly) and it's not bringing in the desired sales, wait until the committed period is over, then distribute it through as many other channels as possible. See what happens. Several authors have achieved phenomenal sales with Barnes & Noble—you may become one of them.

Reader's Choice:
For the price of one traditionally published book, I can get five great indie books.

– Rayne Hall

Book Shop

ARE YOU MISSING OUT ON AMAZON EXPOSURE?

Retailers who want a monopoly on your book offer incentives such as increased exposure or more promotional tools. This applies especially to Amazon.

These opportunities can accelerate your sales. Although for most authors it's best to have many distribution channels, for some, the benefits of making the book exclusive to one are worth it. You won't know until you've tried.

Suggested Action:

Try it for a few months. Make one of your books exclusive to Amazon (or another retailer offering incentives for a temporary monopoly). If sales shoot up, renew the arrangement. If not, relist the book in the other channels.

DO YOU IGNORE SPECIALIST CHANNELS?

Some sales channels are tiny and highly specialised, selling only a few dozen books to a limited number of visitors. Listing your books with them is usually pointless.

But when that seller specialises in your target audience, this can be a wonderful opportunity to build your reputation and boost sales. If you write non-fiction books about puppy training, then a dog lovers' website with a book-selling page is perfect.

Suggested Action:

Identify websites selling books aimed at your target audience. Contact them, suggesting that they stock yours.

IS YOUR BOOK AVAILABLE IN ONLY ONE FORMAT?

Some readers prefer the convenience of ebooks, others prefer a print book's traditional feel. If you know your target audience, you can probably tell to which camp they belong, and make sure you offer your book in the desired format.

But there's more to this than meeting the readers' preference. Books which are available in both electronic and print format get more exposure on book-selling sites. It can be worth having a paperback, even if it doesn't sell a single copy, just to accelerate ebook sales.

Most new authors sell far more ebooks than paperbacks, so make sure your book is available in electronic format.

Perhaps you've shied away from self-publishing print books because of the associated costs. Once upon a time, having a book printed cost a fortune and constituted a big financial risk. But with the print-on-demand (PoD) system, individual books get printed only when a customer orders a copy, at no expense to the author. You simply receive a share of the money whenever a book has been sold.

Suggested Actions:

Publish your book as an ebook. This costs you nothing. If the formatting daunts you, use Draft2Digital where you can upload your manuscript as a docx file and get it turned into mobi and epub formats.

Publish your book as a paperback, even if you don't expect to sell any copies. Use a PoD service.

CreateSpace is practical because it's part of the world's biggest book retailer, Amazon. CreateSpace-published books currently get preferred exposure on Amazon (but don't count on this to always be the case.)

The free templates provided by CreateSpace don't lead to professional-looking books. If you expect to sell many paperbacks, invest in the services of a good formatter who can align the page bottoms and fix other flaws. On the other hand, if you want the paperback purely to increase the ebook's exposure, it doesn't matter what the paperback looks like, and you can save the expense.

MISTAKES I MADE AND LEARNT FROM

Making books exclusive to Amazon for three months, I missed the small print clause that this commitment would be renewed automatically. This small print didn't actually show during the enrolment, I only discovered it afterwards. This was awkward, because I had promotions planned for those books on other sales sites.

CHAPTER 17: FOCUSED EFFORTS ACHIEVE MORE

When a product sells well, it gains attention and receives more exposure, which in turn leads to more sales.

This applies to books even more than to almost any other product because books are displayed in bestseller lists. Once a book is in the top ranks of a bestseller list—even if it's only a book retailer's sub-sub-genre bestseller list—its sales often multiply rapidly.

The higher on the list the book gets, the more exposure it receives, the faster sales figures grow. The beauty of this is that once one of your books becomes popular, readers look for more by the same author, so that one book pulls all your others with it on the upwards spiral of success.

DO YOU SPREAD YOUR RESOURCES ACROSS SEVERAL BOOKS?

You may spend a little of your advertising budget and time on this book, a little on that. That's seldom enough to create a real impact.

If your book climbs from #30 to #3 in its genre, you can expect a drastic, spiralling increase in sales. But if it rises from #3000 to #2000, nothing much happens.

Assuming that your resources of time and money are limited (and for most writers they are), scattering them across several books is ineffective.

Suggested Actions:

Focus all your resources on promoting one book. Choose a book that's already selling reasonably well, so it has a head start, and which is typical for the kind of book you write. This way, it can get into the bestseller lists quickly and pull all your other books with it.

Do everything in your power to increase this book's sales so it climbs in the bestseller lists. Allow this book's success to promote your other books.

This strategy may feel counter-intuitive to the cautious person who hesitates to put all eggs into one basket. Yes, it's a risk, and it may not pay off. The big success may not happen—but there's a realistic change that it will. Whereas if you spread your resources thinly, success will almost certainly elude you.

HAVE YOU SPREAD YOUR RESOURCES OVER A LONG PERIOD?

While continuous intense marketing would be ideal, few authors can afford that. The next best method is concentrated efforts over a short period. These are far more likely to catapult your book into a bestseller list than perpetual tiny dribbles.

Suggested Actions:

Choose the best period for promoting your book. For paperbacks, the weeks before Christmas yield most sales because of gift purchases, while for ebooks, January is a good month. Each genre has its own boom season, for example, horror sells well in the run-up to Halloween.

You have two options. Either pick the period when your type of book sells best, and let the seasonal trends boost your book into the general bestseller lists. Conversely, choose a period when book sales are low and your genre's sales dip. During those weeks, your book may need to sell only a few dozen copies to become one of the top sellers of its genre.

As far as your budget (of time or money) allows, advertise your book in several media at the same time.

Although a short burst of activity is best, resist the temptation to make it a lightning flash. Throwing all your resources into promoting the book for just one day can indeed catapult the book into the bestseller lists—but Amazon's (and other retailers') algorithms are designed to compensate for such flukes, so one-day bursts are spent as fast as fireworks, and then the book drops out of sight.

One month is a good length to choose, but this may differ from genre to genre and month to month, and the constantly changing algorithms don't allow a definite recommendation.

During the promotion period, enlist the help of other authors. Ask them nicely for a plug on their blog or a mention of it in their newsletter. Since it's a one-time request, many will be happy to give their support.

Reader's Choice:
I like ebooks because I don't need to squeeze them into my crowded bookshelves.

- Rayne Hall

CHAPTER 18: CHANGE THE TITLE

The book's title is a major sales tool. Many fiction readers will buy a book spontaneously if the title intrigues. With a non-fiction book, buyers often decide which book to buy based on the title.

If your book doesn't sell as much as it should, change the title. With self-published ebooks, you can change the title in minutes, and the new version will be public in a few days. Print-on-demand also allows title changes without major upheavals. Only if you've used traditional printing methods and invested in a big initial print run would this not be an easy option because of the financial loss.

When changing the title, mention in the book description, "This book was formerly titled [such-and-such]" so readers don't accidentally buy the book twice.

Consider changing the cover at the same time, and maybe making other tweaks, and calling it '2nd revised edition'. This is a useful strategy especially for non-fiction books.

FICTION: DOES THE TITLE FAIL TO REFLECT THE GENRE?

To trigger impulse buys, the title needs to give a clue to the genre. Study the titles of the bestselling novels in your genre, and let them inspire your choice.

Use the thrill words that send genre lover's hearts racing, especially the short evocative ones. Here are some examples.

Thriller: death, dead, die, kill

Western: gun, ride, trail, Texas, trouble, lone, west

Regency Romance: rogue, rake, scandal, bride, lord, lady

Science Fiction: time, world, space

Paranormal Romance: blood, kiss, witch, wolf, moon

Fantasy: quest, mage, sword, song, king

A title containing one or two of these words may make all the difference to your sales.

NON-FICTION: DOES THE TITLE FAIL TO SAY WHAT THE BOOK IS ABOUT?

The best title for a non-fiction book is the one which says exactly what's in the can: *Twitter for Writers. Writing Fight Scenes. How to Get a Job in Germany* (these are all titles of my own books). Such a title is often all the customer needs to decide to buy.

Avoid clever titles which make sense only after reading the book, wordplay and subtle innuendo. Keep it simple.

Consider adding a subtitle to increase the clarity and to catch more keyword searches: *A Concise History. How To [Do Something] Step by Step. Master [Topic] in 30 Days.*

IS YOUR TITLE A COPYCAT?

With hundreds of thousands of new books getting published every year, duplicate titles are inevitable. Don't worry if your title is already in use by an obscure book in a different genre.

But if a currently published book exists with the same title in the same genre, you may want to change yours.

This is especially important for non-fiction. If you use the title of a rival book, you come across as a copycat, and readers may assume you've plagiarised the content.

DOES THE TITLE IMITATE A BESTSELLER

By using a title that is very similar to that of a bestselling work, you can cash in on that book's success. Some readers looking for the bestseller may buy yours by mistake. Some may neglect to check the author name and buy the book in the assumption that it's a sequel to the one they loved. Yet others hope that the similar title indicates similar content and quality.

In the short term, this can be an effective strategy, but in the long term, it may backfire.

Readers whose expectations have been frustrated vent their anger. They may write scathing reviews (and if you get many of those, it will harm sales), and put the author's name on a mental blacklist.

Avoid imitation titles unless your book is a parody or you're interested only in short term sales.

IS THE TITLE TOO LONG?

Short titles have many advantages. You can display them in a huge font size on the cover, and they fit into the shortest promotional messages (such as a 140-character tweet). Online book listings often show only the first 20 or so letters of each title, so your long title will be chopped.

In genre fiction short titles are customary, and genre fans may not take a long title seriously. For Thrillers especially, single-word titles prevail. In literary fiction and non-fiction, longer titles are more acceptable.

CHAPTER 19: THE OPENING SCENE

Many new authors' novels begin with the same few openings.

You may find it hard to believe, but when I was an editor and reading slush piles, eighty per cent of submissions used the same nine beginnings. Sometimes I saw the same opening a dozen times before the day's first coffee break.

Although as an indie author you won't land on an editor's rejection pile, your sample may have the same effect on the reader who downloads samples before deciding which book to buy. Knowing what kind of book she enjoys, she selects a dozen possibles—including yours—and reads the free samples on her Kindle. Her eyes glaze over when she reads the same opening again and again. When she reaches one which is different, she perks up and hits 'buy now'.

Is yours the one which stands out, or one of the same-old?

Here are the overused novel openings which made me yawn when I was an editor, and which these days proliferate among indie-published books.

I've added suggestions how to tweak these beginnings without making major changes, but I can't give you precise instructions because if everyone followed the new recipe it would lead to a new crop of overused beginnings.

1. THE JOURNEY

The character walks/rides/drives/flies/sails to a destination, and on the way reflects on the flora/fauna/history/politics of the place and his own backstory.

Suggested Action:

Cut the journey. Start when he arrives at the destination.

2. THE WARDROBE

The character (usually female) stands in front of her wardrobe and deliberates what to wear for an upcoming event. She may also stand before the mirror, beautifying herself for the event while contemplating her looks.

Suggested Action:

Put another character into the room with her, and let them argue about the upcoming event which has a different significance to each.

3. GETTING OUT OF BED

The character (often a child) wakes in the morning, gets up, brushes teeth, gets dressed and so on, while thinking about the day ahead.

Suggested Action:

Cut that scene. Start with the situation where trouble is brewing and the action is about to begin.

4. CAPTAIN HEARS ALARM

The captain/sergeant/team leader of a military/paramilitary/police/medical/other unit is having a drink with his comrades when suddenly the alarm bell rings. In the resulting scramble, he rallies his team to deal with the emergency.

Suggested Action:

Add a scene before that, showing the captain working on a personal goal. Weave hints of the approaching danger into this scene, as one character senses trouble brewing while another denies it.

5. DISORIENTED WAKE-UP

The character wakes up wondering where he is and how he got there.

Suggested Action:

Start earlier and show how the character got there.

6. WRITER WRITING

The author sits at her computer, thinking about what to write.

Suggested Action:

I hope the story isn't about her fictional characters invading her real life—or you have written the story that almost every other writer has already written. In this case, no amount of clever marketing may help. If the story is about something else, start with the main conflict brewing.

7. THE WINDOW GAZE

The character (usually female) stands or sits at the window, gazing out while ruminating about her situation, her backstory, her father's/husband's/boss's plans, and life in general.

Suggested Action:

Cut that section. The next scene is probably where your novel really starts.

8. WAITING FOR SOMEONE

The character is sitting in a bar/pub/restaurant/club/diner/coffee shop. He is waiting for someone (usually a stranger) whom he is supposed to meet here. The person is delayed.

Suggested Action:

Start with the person already there (unless his delay is due to his death). Change the setting of the scene, so they don't meet in a bar/pub/restaurant/club/diner/coffee shop but an unusual place. Pick the weirdest place where this meeting can plausibly happen, to catch the reader's attention.

9. FOUR LETTER WORDS

"Damn/Fuck//Hell," said the squire/countess/preacher/innkeeper/nun/other character. Many novice authors try to shock the reader to attention by using foul language, but all they achieve is boring the reader who has already read other samples starting the same way.

Suggested Action:

If it's a dialogue scene, start with a line that introduces the conflict. If it's not dialogue, start where something is actually happening or about to happen.

CHAPTER 20: FRESHEN UP YOUR WRITING VOICE

New writers tend to use the same words as almost all other new writers, and they're not aware that they're doing this.

When I was an editor, I could spot a novice's submission by simply glancing at the first two paragraphs. If they contained certain words, I knew this was a beginner who had not developed her unique voice yet.

In the old days, when you submitted your manuscript to publishers for consideration, those words led to automatic rejection. The editors did not tell you the reason, they just attached a standard rejection slip.

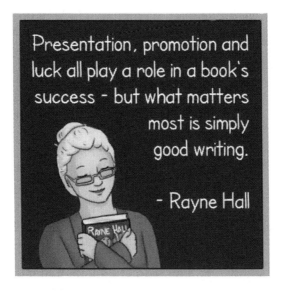

Presentation, promotion and luck all play a role in a book's success - but what matters most is simply good writing.

- Rayne Hall

With indie publishing, your book will not be held back by such gatekeepers, and it passes unhindered to the readers. The average reader perusing samples is unaware of 'novice words', and doesn't use them as a filter—not consciously, that is.

But her subconscious registers that all the samples she's downloaded sound the same, with the same words and phrases. After reading several same-sounding writing samples, her interest perks up when she gets to one with a fresh, original voice.

DO YOU USE NOVICE WORDS?

Here's a list of words novice writers use in their manuscripts. These words are not wrong, but they are not fresh. Several of them on the first page of your sample can doom your book.

Look

turn

could see, could hear, could feel

start to

begin to

sigh

smile

frown

shrug

nod

whisper

exhale

deep breath

slowly

immediately

very

really

completely

Watch especially for combinations of these words, such as 'He/she turned to look at him/her' and 'He/she nodded slowly'.

Suggested Actions:

If your first sample page contains more than three of those words, or if one is repeated, get rid of them at once.

Invest a little time and purge your full sample chapters of these beginner flags.

My earnest recommendation is to eliminate them from your whole book, but this won't be a quick fix. Do it as soon as you can afford the time.

Replace the words with fresher synonyms or original phrases.

Many can be deleted without loss, and this will sharpen your style.

'Turn' and 'look at' are often unnecessary, especially in dialogue where it's implied that the people look at each other while they talk.

'Begin to', 'start to', 'really' and 'could' are also candidates for ruthless cuts:

'She could feel herself beginning to shiver' can be tightened to 'She shivered'.

You'll be surprised how much these simple tweaks can enhance your author voice. Readers perusing fiction samples will appreciate the difference.

MISTAKES I MADE AND LEARNT FROM

My early fiction was full of 'she turned to look at him' and 'he nodded slowly', and I had no idea that these were overused phrases. I thought my writing was brilliant, and was convinced that the editors who rejected it simply lacked insight and taste.

Whenever I stumble across one of those old pieces, I cringe to see all those 'look', 'begin', 'could' and 'nod' words. I'm glad self-publishing was not a viable option for fiction in those days, because I would have published—and regretted it.

DEAR READER,

I hope you enjoyed this book and have found the plugs that block your sales from gushing.

Email me how you got on with this book and which chapters have been most useful to you, and also if you spotted any typos which have escaped the proofreader's eagle eyes. My email address is: rayne_hall_author@yahoo.com. You can also contact me on Twitter: @raynehall.

The cartoon illustrations are by Hanna-Riikka, defcon7a and other artists.

If you find this book helpful, it would be great if you could spread the word about it. Maybe you know other writers who would benefit.

Reviews on sites like Amazon, Barnes & Noble, GoodReads, BookLikes, Smashwords etc. are very welcome. Email me the link to your review, and I'll send you a free review ebook of one of my other Writer's Craft titles. Let me know which one you would like: *Writing Fight Scenes, Writing Scary Scenes, The Word-Loss Diet, Writing About Magic, Writing About Villains, Writing Dark Stories, Writing Short Stories to Promote Your Novels, Twitter for Writers.*

You may want to take a peek at the beginning of *Twitter for Writers* at the end of this book.

With best wishes for writing and publishing success,

Rayne Hall

EXCERPT: TWITTER FOR WRITERS

INTRODUCTION

Writers need different things from Twitter than 'normal' people.

As a writer, you'll use Twitter to meet colleagues, connect with readers, invite reviews, carry out research, improve your writing, develop networks, gain insight, conduct market studies, build your platform, create buzz for your stories, and sell your work.

Twitter is perfect for writers. It's easy to learn, gives you full control of your network, takes less time than other social media, and doesn't bombard you with flashing pop-ups or distracting invitations to play Candy Crush.

"My favourite social network is Twitter. Best interactions, least waste of time."
- Rayne Hall

You can use Twitter as a professional tool without wasting your precious writing time – but be warned,

Twitter can be addictive. In this book, I'll show you how to use Twitter efficiently and to get the greatest benefits in the shortest time.

At the time of writing, I have over 52,000 followers, mostly weird and wonderful writers, and fans of my fiction. Most are real, engaged people who read my tweets and interact, not fake followers and automated accounts. They're also the kind of people who are interested in my books. Some authors have more followers than I – but few have the same quality. The quality of my Twitter 'platform' astonishes marketing experts who sometimes ask me how I do it.

Building this platform took only two years, largely by trial and error, finding out what worked and what did not. By adopting the successful strategies and skipping the mistakes, you can reach similar results even faster.

In this book, I'll show you step by step how you can achieve Twitter success.

I've invented two fictitious writers – Suzie who writes vampire romance novels, and Franco who has published a non-fiction book about dog training – as examples. Adapt my suggestions to suit you. You're the CEO of your Twitter; I'm only the consultant.

You may be new to Twitter, just trying the first steps. Or you may have used Twitter for a while, but aren't really getting anywhere and want to try another approach. You may even be a veteran, looking for advanced techniques to build a platform and promote your books.

For most chapters, I've used this structure: The Basics – What Not To Do – Advanced Strategies - Mistakes I've Made and Learnt From. Read the sections that are relevant for your level and for what you want to achieve. If you're a Twitter novice, stick to The Basics and don't let the

Advanced Strategies overwhelm you. As a seasoned Twitter user, you can skip The Basics and try the Advanced Strategies. If you want a laugh, read the sections about my mistakes.

You can also dip into and out of this book to get the guidance you want right now. The early chapters give the practical essentials; the middle chapters are for when you want to achieve something specific, such as holding a TwitterParty and finding reviewers for your book, while the chapters near the end are more entertaining.

Like everything on the internet, Twitter keeps changing. Much of what I taught in a 'Twitter for Writers' class a year ago is already out of date. By the time you read this book, some details may no longer apply, but the foundation is here for you to build on.

The cartoon illustrations are by several artists, mostly by

Hanna-Riikka who you can follow on Twitter (@DoNichiArt). While you're at it, you can follow me, too (@RayneHall). Tweet me that you're reading this book, and I'll follow you back.

See you on Twitter,

Rayne

CHAPTER 1: CREATING YOUR PROFILE

Go to Twitter.com. If you have an account, log in, and improve it with these tips.

If you're new, create an account. For this, you'll need to provide some personal details and an email address. You'll be asked to follow some big organisations and famous people before you're allowed to proceed. Just click some at random. You can unfollow them later.

THE BASICS

Don't worry about getting things perfect at this stage. If you change your mind about something, you can make changes.

Full Name and User Name

Both your 'Full Name' and your 'User Name' show up frequently and play an important part in your branding and promotion.

I recommend you use your pen name (the author name of your books) for both. This will help a lot with book marketing and search engine optimisation. You may not care about those things yet, but one day they may become tremendously important. Securing your pen name as your User Name now will help you sell books in the future.

For the Full Name, use it exactly as you use it for your books. Let's say you write under the pen name Suzie Scrybe. Then you would use Suzie Scrybe as your Full Name on Twitter – not Suzie Z. Scrybe, S. Scrybe or Miss Scrybe.

For the User Name, pick your pen name as well. However, this time you can't use spaces. Suzie Scrybe is @SuzieScrybe. On Twitter, your user name is always preceded by the '@' symbol.

If your pen name is already taken (that's quite possible), see if you can add punctuation marks. For example, Suzie's user name may be @Suzie_Scrybe or @SuzieScrybe_. You could also add a word, for example @SuzieScrybeBook.

Long pen names are problematic, because Twitter allows only 15 letters for a user name. If you write under the name Clarabella Dorothea Watkins-Himmelreich, you may have to limit your user name to @Himmelreich.

Password

Pick something other people can't guess – not the title of your book. The ideal Password is long and includes punctuation marks and numbers, for example *))King989Arthur((* or *^&3Little^&3Dipper*. Don't use the same Password you use for online banking or other social media.

Write it down somewhere you can access it, but not where hackers can. Change it several times a year.

If you ever suspect your account has been hacked, change the Password at once.

Profile Picture

Your Profile Picture is called an 'avatar' ('avi' for short). Upload one as soon as you create your account. Unless you have a picture, other Twitter users will hold you in contempt or suspect you to be not a real person but a robot. If you don't have a picture that's quite right, upload whatever you have at hand now. You can change it later.

The most effective avatar is a portrait of yourself.

If you don't like to display your photo, use a drawing or painting. Go to OCAL (Open Clipart Library) search 'woman face' or 'man face', pick one that looks a bit like you, download it, and upload it as your Twitter profile picture. OCAL pictures are copyright-free. The drawback is that someone else could be using the same picture.

You could also get an artist to paint an 'artist's impression' of you. This can be realistic or a cartoon. Use intense colours, not pastels. Perhaps someone in your family or circle of friends can do it for you for free. Or you can hire a cartoonist or illustrator, either a hobbyist, an aspiring professional or a professional. Expect to pay between $5 and $50. You can then use the same picture for other purposes, such as your Facebook profile and your Amazon Author Central page.

Don't use a full-body picture, or a picture showing you with hubby, pet or other people. The profile pic will be displayed so small, anything more than the head doesn't work.

A portrait that reflects your genre is best - unless you write erotica. Then it's best to avoid anything sexy, or Twitter users will mistake you for a porn spammer.

If you have books published, consider uploading the cover of your most important book instead of a picture of yourself. This creates potentially huge exposure for your cover, and your followers will see that cover so often that subconsciously they perceive it as a bestselling book. However, the Twitter Profile Picture is square and small. I recommend creating a new picture with a square-cropped part of the cover picture, and the book title pasted into it. Ask a digital design-savvy friend to do this for you. The drawback is that every tweet you send will look like an advertisement, and most people are fed up with seeing advertising everywhere.

Profile Text

Definitely fill in the profile text. That's how people will identify you as an interesting person whose tweets they want to read. You have up to 160 characters.

Don't waste the words on meaningless drivel, and don't try to be overly clever. Use words which will help like-minded people (and readers!) find you.

I recommend you simply say what you write. This will help a lot with marketing and promotion. Use the combination of 'Writer' or 'Author' and your genre(s) or subgenres, for example, 'Paranormal Romance Author'. These three words are all you need. They'll serve you well on Twitter. People who're interested in paranormal romance will find you – and this is your main aim on Twitter.

You can also add search words, based on your interests and what you will tweet about. I recommend using words related to your novels, with or without #hashtags. (More about hashtags in Chapter 6.)

Paragraph breaks don't work in the profile text.

Here are examples:

Rayne Hall

Author & editor of fantasy & horror. Writer's Craft books: Writing Fight Scenes, Writing About Magic, Writing Scary Scenes, Writing Dark Stories & more.

Suzie Scrybe

Suzie Scrybe is a paranormal romance author who loves reading and writing about vampires.

Franco Folly

Author of 'The Zen of Dog Training' & 'Train Your Dog at Home – The Buddhist Way'. #dogs #puppies #buddhism #pets

Notifications

Every time someone follows, favourites, tweets or retweets you or a tweet you were mentioned in, Twitter sends you an email, which soon becomes a nuisance. Twitter also emails you with information about services you can buy. To avoid getting inundated with junk emails, do this:

Click the cogwheel symbol at the top. Click 'Settings', click 'Notifications'. Uncheck every Notification. You can change the settings later if you wish.

WHAT NOT TO DO

For your profile picture, avoid using cute animals. Thousands of people on Twitter use pictures of cats and dogs; people won't be able to tell you apart. Use animal pictures in your tweets instead.

Also stay away from pictures of objects, especially typewriters, piles of books, quills and book pages shaped into hearts: so many writers use those as their profile picture, you'll just get lost among many.

Some people use complex code to create Twitter avatars that change, rotate or flash, in hopes of getting attention – but the result looks like annoying advertising, and people hate it.

Don't waste your profile text on useless drivel such as 'If you want to find out about me, read my tweets' or '160 characters is not enough to express who I am'.

Some people's profile text says 'This is the official Twitter account of...' pretending that they're celebrities. You'll become a laughing-stock if you do.

Don't reveal personal information in your profile text.

Don't brag in your profile text. 'Bestselling Author' comes across as hyperbolic and desperate. The genuine bestselling authors don't use such claims.

ADVANCED STRATEGIES

You can change your profile text at any time. The avatar can be changed, too, but not from every device.

In the fast-moving world of Twitter, people will spot your avatar before they notice your name. This is how they recognise you. The familiarity of your avatar is a huge advantage, so avoid changing it.

If you want to experiment with different avatars, do it at the early stages, before you have many followers and before people are accustomed to associating a particular picture with you.

If your branding strategy involves specific colours – perhaps all your book covers are pink – then it can be a good idea to make pink the dominant colour of your avatar. You can further the visual brand recognition by using the same picture for all social media accounts and your website.

You can add further visual elements to your profile, for example, add a 'header' picture and select or create a background wallpaper. Many writers choose their book covers for the wallpaper and click 'tile' so the same picture is repeated over and over. However, these will not be viewed as much as your avatar, and you can skip them if you want to save time.

If you enjoy changing pictures around frequently, play with your header and wallpaper, but keep your avatar consistent.

If you are interested in SEO (search engine optimisation)

include your pen name as part of your profile text. 'Suzie Scrybe is a paranormal romance author.' This may look odd if it's directly under your user name, but it helps with search engine optimisation.

Another way to boost SEO is to change the profile text frequently by adding, removing and rearranging words.

However, for the average author, SEO is not a major concern, you may not want to bother.

MISTAKES I MADE AND LEARNT FROM

When I started, I chose an avatar based on the cover of my dark epic fantasy novel *Storm Dancer*, which I wanted to promote at the time.

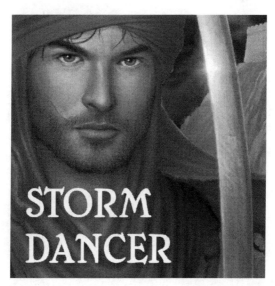

Since the cover features a man, people assumed that Rayne Hall was male, and were startled to learn that I'm female. Many imagined that the bloke on the cover was Rayne Hall, and some women tried to flirt.

The book cover as avatar also looked like an advertisement instead of a real person.

After a year, I wanted to change the picture. But by now, I had acquired a huge following who recognised my avatar, and with it an enormous visual brand recognition. I didn't want to throw that advantage away.

Another year passed, during which I gained yet more followers and more brand recognition, and I wished I had changed the avatar long ago. The longer I waited, the more I had to lose.

Eventually, I decided to just do it. Now I'm using this picture:

It's an artist's impression (by Fawnheart) of what I look like, and it's in my brand colours of blue and turquoise, similar to the cartoons and the Writer's Craft book covers. If you look closely, you can see that she painted half of me 'undead', a clever allusion to the kind of stories I write, although this detail is not noticeable at the size normally seen on Twitter.

To smooth the transition, I tweeted for a couple of weeks that I would soon have a new avatar, using the blue picture as an attachment. After the change, I tweeted several times, *I've changed my avatar. New picture, same person, still real*, and attached the old one.

I tweeted these so often that some of my regular followers got bored with the announcement – but others still were confused by the change.

(end of sample)

Made in the USA
San Bernardino, CA
19 June 2015